THE BALTIMORE ORIOLES

BY

MARK STEWART

NORWOOD HOUSE PRESS

CHICAGO, ILLINOIS

Norwood House Press
P.O. Box 316598
Chicago, Illinois 60631

For information regarding Norwood House Press, please visit our website at:
www.norwoodhousepress.com or call 866-565-2900.

All photos courtesy of Getty Images except the following:
Tom DiPace (4, 11, 14, 35 bottom, 36), Golden Press (6), SportsChrome (8, 10),
Topps, Inc. (9, 15, 16, 31 bottom, 34 top, 38, 42 top), Gum Inc. (20), The Sporting News (22, 41),
Black Book Partners Archives (23, 26, 36, 39, 40, 43 top, 45), Macfadden Publications (28),
A.M. Briggs & Co. (30), Ziv Television Productions (31 top), Baltimore Orioles (33, 34 bottom left, 42 bottom),
Sweet Caporal (34 bottom right), Author's Collection (43 left), Matt Richman (48).
Cover Photo: Rob Carr/Getty Images

The memorabilia and artifacts pictured in this book are presented for educational and informational purposes,
and come from the collection of the author.

Editor: Mike Kennedy
Designer: Ron Jaffe
Project Management: Black Book Partners, LLC.
Special thanks to Topps, Inc.

Library of Congress Cataloging-in-Publication Data

Stewart, Mark, 1960-
The Baltimore Orioles / by Mark Stewart. -- Library ed.
     p. cm. -- (Team spirit)
   Summary: "A Team Spirit Baseball edition featuring the Baltimore Orioles
that chronicles the history and accomplishments of the team. Includes
bibliographical references and index. Includes access to the Team Spirit
website, which provides additional information, updates and photos"--Provided
by publisher.
   ISBN 978-1-59953-474-9 (library : alk. paper) -- ISBN 978-1-60357-354-2
(ebook) 1. Baltimore Orioles (Baseball team)--History--Juvenile
literature. I. Title.
   GV875.B2S74 2012
   796.357'640975271--dc23

                                            2011048204

Manufactured in the United States of America in North Mankato, Minnesota.
196N—012012

COVER PHOTO: The Orioles jump for joy after a win in 2011.

TABLE OF CONTENTS

ABOUT OUR GLOSSARY

In this book, there may be several words that you are reading for the first time. Some are sports words, some are new vocabulary words, and some are familiar words that are used in an unusual way. All of these words are defined on page 46. Throughout the book, sports words appear in **bold type**. Regular vocabulary words appear in ***bold italic type***.

MEET THE ORIOLES

I n many parts of the United States, the return of the oriole signals the start of spring. In Baltimore, Maryland, the return of the Orioles means it is time for a new baseball season to begin. The team has been an important part of life in this region of the country going back *generations*. The Orioles have played in the city longer than any other sports team.

Many baseball fans are surprised to learn about the twists and turns in the Orioles' history. Indeed, the team played under other names and in other cities before arriving in town during the 1950s. But ever since, they have been what Baltimore sports is all about.

This book tells the story of the Orioles. There is something about the orange and black of the Baltimore uniform that brings out the fight in a baseball player. The Orioles play hard and never let up. They are loud and proud and full of energy.

Adam Jones heads for the dugout after scoring a run. The Orioles cheer for one another at all times.

The history of baseball in Baltimore stretches back into the 1800s. A team called the Orioles has played in Baltimore for almost all of that time. The New York Yankees were called the Baltimore Orioles once.

Today's Orioles actually got their start in Milwaukee, Wisconsin. The year was 1901, and the **American League (AL)** was playing its first season. One of the eight teams in the AL was the Milwaukee

GEORGE SISLER
first base

Brewers. After one year, the Brewers moved to St. Louis and were renamed the Browns. They signed some of the best players from the crosstown Cardinals, including Jack Powell, Bobby Wallace, and Jesse Burkett.

The Browns played in St. Louis for more than 50 years. During that time they had several good players, including George Sisler, Ken Williams, Del Pratt, Harlond Clift, and Jack Tobin. In 1922, the Browns nearly won the **pennant**.

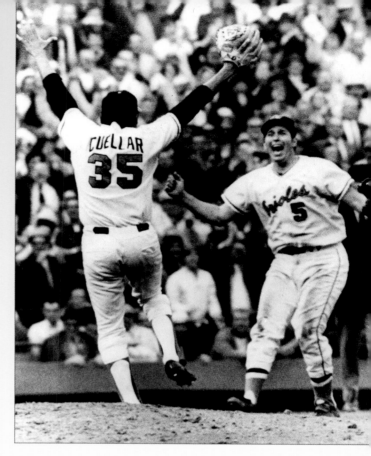

In 1944, they finally captured their first league championship. Unfortunately, the World Series was a disappointment. The Browns were beaten by their St. Louis "neighbors," the Cardinals.

By the early 1950s, there simply was not enough room in St. Louis for two teams. The Browns moved to Baltimore in 1954 and took the name Orioles. They have been there ever since.

The Orioles lost 100 games in their first season in Baltimore, but the losing would not last long. The team spent a lot of money and time developing new players. Baltimore's first big star was Brooks Robinson. He was the best defensive third baseman anyone had ever seen. Robinson could hit, too. In 1964, Robinson led the AL in **runs batted in (RBIs)** and was named the league's **Most Valuable Player (MVP)**.

Robinson was joined by other talented players in the 1960s, including Boog Powell, Paul Blair, Milt Pappas, Steve Barber, Wally Bunker, Jim Palmer, Mike Cuellar, and Dave McNally. By 1966, the team had added superstars Frank Robinson and Luis Aparicio to the lineup. The Orioles won the pennant and defeated the Los Angeles Dodgers in the World Series that season. In 1968, Baltimore hired Earl Weaver to manage the team. He won four more pennants over the next 12 years.

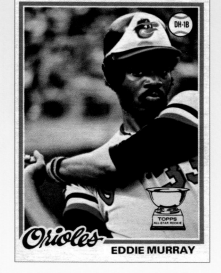

By the 1980s, the names and faces had changed in Baltimore, but the winning *tradition* continued. The club was now led by Cal Ripken Jr. and Eddie Murray. Ripken would become one of the greatest and most popular players in history. From 1982 to 1998, he played in 2,632 games in a row. Ripken would one day go into the **Hall of Fame**. Murray also had a great career and joined his teammate there.

In 1992, the Orioles moved into beautiful new Oriole Park at Camden Yards. More than two million fans came to watch the team play every year. They rooted for Ripken and his talented teammates, including Mike Mussina, Roberto Alomar, Rafael Palmeiro, Brady Anderson, Scott Erickson, and Randy Myers.

LEFT: Cal Ripken Jr. set a record by playing in 2,632 games in a row.
ABOVE: Eddie Murray hit more than 300 home runs as an Oriole.

In 1996 and 1997, the Orioles came close to returning to the World Series. They reached the **American League Championship Series (ALCS)** both years. However, they were unable to take the final step and win another pennant.

The Orioles relied on Ripken as long as they could. He played 21 seasons for Baltimore and set a high standard for the team leaders who followed him. When it came time to rebuild, Baltimore turned to experienced players. They included Melvin Mora, Miguel Tejada, Mark Reynolds, and Vladimir Guerrero. The team also developed many young stars, such as Brian Roberts, Adam Jones, Nick Markakis, and Matt Weiters.

The Orioles play in the **AL East** with the New York Yankees, Boston Red Sox, Toronto Blue Jays, and Tampa Bay Rays. The

competition is fierce. To finish first, a team needs to have good hitting and pitching. The Orioles have never had trouble finding talented hitters. Their home field is very friendly to players who have power and drive in runs. Pitching is harder to come by.

As the Orioles move into the future, they look to the glory days of their clubs from the 1960s, 1970s, and 1980s. A great team starts with a solid pitching staff. Once good hitters are added to the mix, winning becomes easier and easier.

LEFT: Brian Roberts
ABOVE: Nick Markakis

HOME TURF

For their first 38 seasons, the Orioles played in Baltimore's Memorial Stadium. In 1992, the team moved into Oriole Park at Camden Yards—or simply "Camden Yards," as fans call it. The stadium is just two blocks from the birthplace of Babe Ruth, who grew up in Baltimore and played for an early minor-league team called the Orioles. Ruth's father ran a café on Conway Street, which is now part of the center field stands.

The company that created Camden Yards studied baseball's most famous ballparks, including Wrigley Field, Fenway Park, Ebbets Field, and the Polo Grounds. The builders mixed the best of these old stadiums with many new ideas. Since Camden Yards opened, several other teams have built stadiums mixing old and new.

BY THE NUMBERS

- The Orioles' stadium has 45,480 seats.
- The distance from home plate to the left field foul pole is 333 feet.
- The distance from home plate to the center field fence is 400 feet.
- The distance from home plate to the right field foul pole is 318 feet.

Fans cheer for the Orioles at Camden Yards.

As long as they have been in Baltimore, the Orioles have worn black and orange, the colors of the bird for which they were named. The team has used an oriole on its cap every season, except for a short while in the 1960s. During that time, they switched to an orange letter *B* for hats worn at home games.

In some years, the Orioles' cap *logo* has looked like a real bird. In others, it has been a cartoon. Several different artists have drawn Baltimore's oriole, including Stan Walsh. He was famous for creating the breakfast cereal characters Snap, Crackle, and Pop.

The team has worn many different uniforms over the years, but always with the color combination of orange, black, and white. In the early 1970s, the Orioles sometimes wore orange bottoms and tops at the same time! In recent years, they used a black jersey and also a bright orange jersey on special occasions.

LEFT: Adam Jones wears the Orioles' 2011 road uniform.   **ABOVE**: This 1964 trading card shows Boog Powell in a uniform similar to the 2011 version. In 2012, the team changed back to a cartoon bird on its caps.

WE WON!

The difference between a good team and a championship team can be a single player. That was the case in 1966, when the Orioles traded for Frank Robinson. Baltimore already had excellent pitching, speed, and defense, but the club needed one more big bat in the lineup. Robinson gave the team the help it needed by

winning the AL **Triple Crown** and MVP award. He combined with Boog Powell and Brooks Robinson to hit more than 100 home runs, and the Orioles won the pennant by nine games.

Baltimore faced the Los Angeles Dodgers in the World Series. Most fans thought the Dodgers would win. They had two of the best pitchers in baseball, Sandy Koufax and Don Drysdale. In Game 1, the Orioles scored four runs in the first two innings against Drysdale. When the Dodgers scored twice to make the score 4–2, Baltimore manager Hank Bauer brought in Moe Drabowsky to pitch

in the third inning. Drabowsky finished the game and struck out 11 batters. The Orioles won 5–2.

Amazingly, the Dodgers would not score again. The next afternoon, 20-year-old Jim Palmer beat Koufax 6–0. Two days later, in Baltimore, Wally Bunker took the mound for the Orioles and threw a 1–0 **shutout**. Dave McNally finished off the Dodgers in Game 4 with another 1–0 shutout. The Orioles had their first championship.

LEFT: Frank Robinson
ABOVE: The Orioles celebrate their 1966 World Series championship.

Baltimore won more than 100 games in 1969 and returned to the World Series. Unfortunately, the Orioles lost to the New York Mets. They suffered the same fate in 1971, when the Pittsburgh Pirates beat them in the World Series. The 1970 season was a different story. The Orioles faced the Cincinnati Reds in the World Series and won in five games. Brooks Robinson was the star of this series. He made one great fielding play after another and batted .429. McNally also chipped in on the mound. He threw a **complete game** and hit the

LEFT: Brooks Robinson dives for a ball during the 1970 World Series.
RIGHT: Rick Dempsey waves to the crowd during the team's victory parade in 1983.

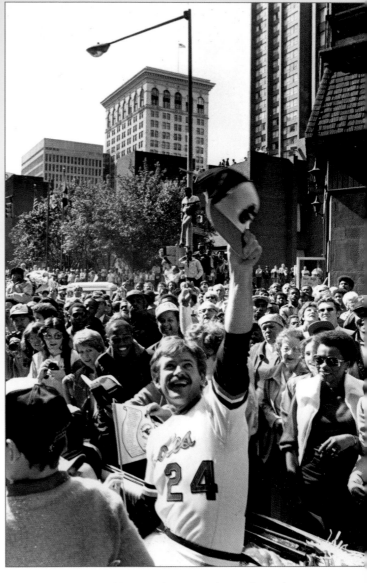

first **grand slam** by a pitcher in a World Series.

The Orioles lost a rematch with the Pirates in the 1979 World Series. They played for the championship again in 1983 against the Philadelphia Phillies. After losing the opener, Baltimore came back to win three games in a row. The Orioles took Game 5 to win their third championship. The pitching stars included Scott McGregor, Mike Flanagan, Mike Boddicker, Tippy Martinez, and Palmer—the same player who had beaten the Dodgers 17 years earlier! The man calling the pitches for the Orioles was catcher Rick Dempsey. He was known mostly for his defense, but he batted .385 and was voted World Series MVP.

GO-TO GUYS

To be a true star in baseball, you need more than a quick bat and a strong arm. You have to be a "go-to guy"—someone the manager wants on the pitcher's mound or in the batter's box when it matters most. Fans of the Browns and Orioles have had a lot to cheer about over the years, including these great stars …

THE PIONEERS

GEORGE SISLER   First Baseman

• BORN: 3/24/1893   • DIED: 3/26/1973   • PLAYED FOR TEAM: 1915 TO 1927

George Sisler was a great college pitcher when he joined the Browns. But his hitting was so good that the team moved him to first base. He won two batting championships and led the AL in stolen bases four times.

HARLOND CLIFT

HARLOND CLIFT   Third Baseman

• BORN: 8/12/1912   • DIED: 4/27/1992

• PLAYED FOR TEAM: 1934 TO 1943

Harlond Clift was one of baseball's first power-hitting third basemen. His keen batting eye helped him draw more than 100 walks six times in his career. Clift was the Browns' best player in the 1930s.

BROOKS ROBINSON   Third Baseman

• BORN: 5/18/1937   • PLAYED FOR TEAM: 1955 TO 1977

Brooks Robinson was the starting third baseman in the **All-Star Game** 15 years in a row. He was such a good fielder that he was nicknamed the "Human Vacuum Cleaner." Robinson was the league MVP in 1964, All-Star Game MVP in 1966, and World Series MVP in 1970.

JIM PALMER   Pitcher

• BORN: 10/15/1945

• PLAYED FOR TEAM: 1965 TO 1967 & 1969 TO 1984

Jim Palmer overcame control problems and a sore arm to capture the **Cy Young Award** three times for the Orioles in the 1970s. His high leg-kick and over-the-top throwing style helped him win 20 or more games eight times from 1970 to 1978.

FRANK ROBINSON   Outfielder

• BORN: 8/31/1935   • PLAYED FOR TEAM: 1966 TO 1971

The Cincinnati Reds traded Frank Robinson to the Orioles because they thought he was too old. Robinson proved them wrong by winning the Triple Crown in his first season with Baltimore and leading the team to its first championship. He hit 179 home runs during his six years as an Oriole.

LEFT: Harlond Clift   **ABOVE**: Jim Palmer

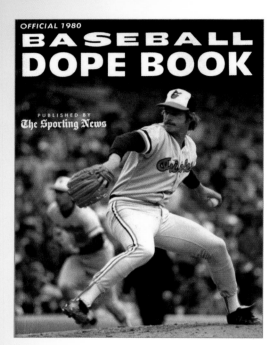

MIKE FLANAGAN — Pitcher

- BORN: 12/16/1951
- DIED: 8/24/2011
- PLAYED FOR TEAM: 1975 to 1987 & 1991 to 1992

Mike Flanagan was one of baseball's most dependable players. From 1977 to 1987, no pitcher in the AL started more games. Flanagan had a marvelous curveball and specialized in picking off runners who wandered too far from first base.

EDDIE MURRAY — First Baseman

- BORN: 2/24/1956
- PLAYED FOR TEAM: 1977 to 1988 & 1996

Eddie Murray was the most fearsome **switch-hitter** of his day. He was at his best with runners on base, and especially dangerous with the bases loaded. Murray also won the Gold Glove three times for his excellent fielding.

CAL RIPKEN JR. — Shortstop/Third Baseman

- BORN: 8/24/1960
- PLAYED FOR TEAM: 1981 to 2001

Cal Ripken Jr. was the heart and soul of the Orioles for two *decades*. He won two AL MVP awards and finished his career with more than 3,000 hits and 400 home runs.

ABOVE: Mike Flanagan   **RIGHT**: Mike Mussina

MIKE MUSSINA   Pitcher

• BORN: 12/8/1968

• PLAYED FOR TEAM: 1991 TO 2000

Mike Mussina used a darting fastball and a strange "knuckle-curve" to become the team's best pitcher in the 1990s. He won 147 games for the Orioles and led Baltimore in victories six times.

NICK MARKAKIS   Outfielder

• BORN: 11/17/1983

• FIRST YEAR WITH TEAM: 2006

Nick Markakis joined the Orioles in 2006 and became the team's top hitter a year later. In 2007, he batted .300 and led Baltimore in doubles, home runs, and RBIs.

ADAM JONES   Outfielder

• BORN: 8/1/1985

• FIRST YEAR WITH TEAM: 2008

The Orioles traded for Adam Jones because they thought he could be an All-Star. They were right. In 2009, Jones played in the All-Star Game and knocked in the winning run for the AL. He also won a Gold Glove that year.

CALLING THE SHOTS

The Orioles and their fans have always taken great pride in the leaders who work in the Baltimore dugout. Since its earliest days, the team has hired brilliant baseball men. The first was Paul Richards. He built the Orioles into a winner with smart trades. He also gave talented teenagers such as Brooks Robinson and Milt Pappas a chance to shine.

The first manager to lead Baltimore to a championship was Hank Bauer. He had been a member of the great New York Yankees teams of the 1950s. Bauer had also been a soldier in *World War II* and won medals for his bravery. Bauer always had the respect of his "troops." The Orioles have had other fine managers, including Davey Johnson, Joe Altobelli, Cal Ripken Sr., and Johnny Oates.

The most successful manager in team history was Earl Weaver. He led the team to six first-place finishes in the AL East and four pennants. Baltimore had only one losing season with Weaver in charge. He liked to say that his job was simple. He filled his lineup with power hitters, sent good pitchers to the mound, and asked

Earl Weaver shows his plaque at the Hall of Fame in Cooperstown, New York. He was honored by the museum in 1996.

his defense to avoid errors. Of course, there was a lot more to Weaver's winning **strategy**.

In his office, Weaver kept stacks of notebooks filled with statistics. He knew how every one of his hitters did against every single pitcher—and how every one of his pitchers did against every single hitter. Fans would scratch their heads when they saw a weak hitter such as Mark Belanger placed high in the batting order. They thought Weaver was crazy when he would bench sluggers such as Boog Powell or Frank Robinson. Long before managers used computers, Weaver knew that the numbers told an important story. More often than not, he was right.

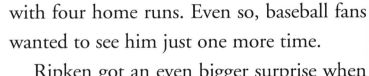

No one was more surprised than 40-year-old Cal Ripken Jr. when all the fan votes for the 2001 All-Star Game were counted. He had been chosen as the AL's starting third baseman. Ripken was playing in his final season, and he was batting only .240 with four home runs. Even so, baseball fans wanted to see him just one more time.

Ripken got an even bigger surprise when he trotted out to his position to start the first inning. Alex Rodriguez walked over to him and shoved him toward his old position at shortstop, where he had once started 12 All-Star games in a row. Rodriguez played third base in his place. A lot of baseball fans had tears in their eyes after this touching gesture.

The tears returned two innings later, when Ripken walked to the plate. The

LEFT: Cal Ripken Jr. completes a double play during his days as an All-Star shortstop.
RIGHT: Ripken slugs Chan Ho Park's pitch toward the left field stands in the 2001 All-Star Game.

fans rose to their feet and gave him a long ovation. No sooner had the crowd quieted down than Ripken slammed the first pitch he saw from Chan Ho Park into the left field stands for a home run.

In the sixth inning, Ripken was taken out of the game. Play was stopped while a short ceremony was held to honor him. Every player on both teams came out to congratulate him on his great career.

The AL went on to win 4–1. Ripken was selected as the game's MVP. He had won the award before, in 1991. No one else in AL history had done this twice. "Cal comes up, sees one pitch, and hits a home run off a pitcher he has probably never seen before," said an amazed Randy Johnson, who was an All-Star teammate of Ripken's for many years. "That's the kind of magic that Cal brings to the field, that he's brought to the field for twenty years."

LEGEND HAS IT

WHO INVENTED THE 'PANCAKE' GLOVE?

LEGEND HAS IT that Paul Richards did. The Baltimore manager was tired of watching his catchers miss the

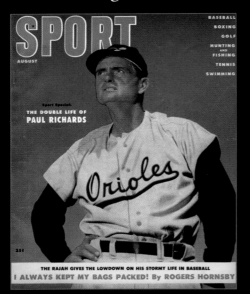

knuckleballs thrown by his star pitcher, Hoyt Wilhelm. In 1960, he ordered gigantic flat gloves to be made, so that it would be easier to block these dipping, darting pitches. The first "pancake" glove measured almost 16 inches across and 50 inches in *circumference*. Today, catcher's mitts can be no larger than 38 inches in circumference. In the end, Richards decided to trade Wilhelm to the Chicago White Sox for shortstop Luis Aparicio, who would help the Orioles win their first pennant. "You just don't want a knuckleballer pitching for you," Richards admitted. Of course, he added, "You don't want one pitching against you, either!"

WHO WAS BALTIMORE'S MOST UNUSUAL RELIEF PITCHER?

LEGEND HAS IT that Don Stanhouse was. Off the field, Stanhouse had a crazy hairstyle, often screamed for no reason, and thought of himself as an elegant gentleman. On the mound, he worked very slowly and walked a lot of batters. Yet somehow, he usually managed to squirm out of trouble. Stanhouse was given the perfect nickname: Stan the Man Unusual.

WHO WAS THE HARDEST-THROWING PITCHER THE ORIOLES EVER SIGNED?

LEGEND HAS IT that Steve Dalkowski was. Dalkowski's nickname was "White Lightning," and his fastball hissed toward the batter with terrifying speed. But like lightning, you never knew where it would strike. Many experts estimated that Dalkowski could throw the ball at nearly 110 miles per hour. Unfortunately, he could not control his pitches, and the Orioles never called him up from the minor leagues.

In the early years of the Orioles, Paul Richards oversaw the team's business off the field. Richards was a very good judge of talent. He was told that he could spend whatever was needed to build a good team. However, when Baltimore's owner saw the team's budget grow to nearly three times what he expected, Richards had new orders: make some trades.

A couple of months after the Orioles' first season ended in 1954, Richards announced a blockbuster. The Orioles traded a total of 18 players with the New York Yankees. Baltimore parted with pitchers Don Larsen and Bob Turley, along with five other players. In return, the Orioles got Gus Triandos, Gene Woodling, and nine more players.

The "super trade" worked out well for both teams. Triandos became an All-Star catcher who helped develop young Baltimore

DON LARSEN, Pitcher
Born: August 7, 1929
Hometown: San Diego, Calif.
Throws Right — Bats Right

GUS TRIANDOS
BALTIMORE ORIOLES

pitchers for many years. Turley and Larsen pitched well for the Yankees.

Woodling struggled at first for the Orioles and was traded away during the 1955 season. Baltimore got him back a few years later, and this time he played much better. Woodling's best season with the Orioles was 1959. That year, he batted .300 with 14 homers and 77 RBIs. He also became an All-Star for the only time in his career.

In 1956, meanwhile, Richards nearly outdid himself. Early in the season, he proposed a whopper of a deal with the Kansas City A's. Richards wanted to exchange all 25 players on his roster for the 25 players on Kansas City's roster. The A's thought long and hard about the offer, but they turned it down in the end.

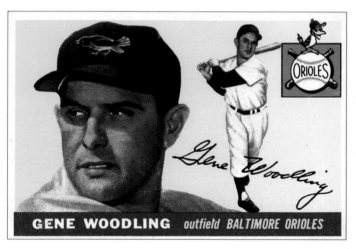

GENE WOODLING *outfield BALTIMORE ORIOLES*

TEAM SPIRIT

Baseball is a family affair in Baltimore. Many of the young fans in the seats at Orioles games are the children, grandchildren, or even great-grandchildren of people who grew up rooting for the team. Since the Orioles moved to Camden Yards in the 1990s, a trip to the stadium often includes a visit to the Baltimore Aquarium or a stroll along the city's beautiful waterfront.

The Orioles make a point of strengthening their bond with the fans. The players do, too. They can be seen all over the area. They visit schools, camps, hospitals, and businesses. Of course, nothing could ever top the day that Cal Ripken Jr. set the record for most games played in a row. He circled the entire stadium and gave fans high-fives as they cheered his remarkable achievement.

LEFT: Cal Ripken Jr. reaches out to Orioles fans after becoming baseball's new "Iron Man."   **ABOVE**: Baltimore fans bought this yearbook in 1954, the team's first season.

TIMELINE

This pin was sold at the ballpark in 1954.

1954
The team moves to Baltimore and becomes the Orioles.

1973
Al Bumbry is named **Rookie of the Year**.

1902
The St. Louis Browns play their first season.

1966
The Orioles win their first World Series.

1980
Steve Stone wins the Cy Young Award.

Bobby Wallace was the Browns' first big star.

WALLACE, ST. LOUIS, AMER.

The Orioles celebrate their victory in 1966.

WORLD SERIES GAME #4

ORIOLES WIN 4TH STRAIGHT

BALT.: 1
L.A.: 0

Cal Ripken Jr. is honored at Camden Yards.

1995
Cal Ripken Jr. sets a record by playing in 2,131 games in a row.

2011
Matt Weiters wins his first Gold Glove.

1983
The Orioles win their third World Series.

1992
Oriole Park at Camden Yards opens.

2007
Brian Roberts leads the AL with 50 steals.

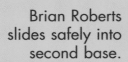

Brian Roberts slides safely into second base.

FUN FACTS

NICE JOB, ROOKIE

In 1978, Sammy Stewart pitched his first game for the Orioles, against the Chicago White Sox. He set a record by striking out the first seven batters he faced.

WHO'S ON FIRST?

The Orioles had two of baseball's most powerful first basemen in the 1960s. In 1961, Jim Gentile set a team record with five grand slams. Boog Powell hit more than 30 homers three times during the decade.

NONSTOP SHORTSTOP

During his five seasons in Baltimore, Miguel Tejada set team records with 214 hits (2006) and 150 RBIs (2004). "Miggy" also led the AL in **assists** twice.

ABOVE: Miguel Tejada
RIGHT: The Ripken family—Billy, Cal Sr., and Cal Jr.

LIKE FATHER, LIKE SONS

In 1987, Cal Ripken Sr. was the manager of the Orioles. His sons—second baseman Billy and shortstop Cal Jr.—made up his double play combination.

GO TO BED, BRIAN!

From 2003 to 2005, Brian Roberts and B.J. Surhoff were teammates on the Orioles. Years earlier, Surhoff had been Roberts's babysitter.

FOUR ACES

In 1971, the Orioles had four 20-game winners on their pitching staff. Dave McNally won 21 games, and Mike Cuellar, Jim Palmer, and Pat Dobson each won 20.

"For all of your support over the years, I want to thank you, the fans of Baltimore, from the bottom of my heart. This is the greatest place to play."

▶ *CAL RIPKEN JR., TO THE PEOPLE OF BALTIMORE*

"On my tombstone just write, 'The sorest loser that ever lived.'"

▶ *EARL WEAVER, ON HIS PASSION FOR WINNING*

"If you're not practicing, somebody else is somewhere, and he'll be ready to take your job."

▶ *BROOKS ROBINSON, ON THE IMPORTANCE OF HARD WORK*

ABOVE: Brooks Robinson
RIGHT: Rick Dempsey

"It's about winning. If you can tell somebody something and it can help the team, that's what you do."
▶ **EDDIE MURRAY**, *ON BEING A TEAM PLAYER*

"Losing is no disgrace if you've given your best."
▶ **JIM PALMER**, *ON HOW TO HANDLE A LOSS WITH GRACE*

"He never quit—this guy never quit."
▶ **RICK DEMPSEY**, *ON TEAMMATE MIKE FLANAGAN*

"I'm not satisfied, I'm never satisfied."
▶ **ADAM JONES**, *ON HIS DESIRE TO IMPROVE AS A PLAYER*

GREAT DEBATES

People who root for the Browns and Orioles love to compare their favorite moments, teams, and players. Some debates have been going on for years! How would you settle these classic baseball arguments?

DON BUFORD WAS BALTIMORE'S BEST LEADOFF HITTER ...

... because as the first batter in the lineup, he "set the table" for the sluggers behind him. Buford was a good hitter, fast runner, and an expert at getting on base. When the Orioles toured Japan one year, he was called "The Greatest Leadoff Man in the World." In 1969, Buford led off the World Series with a home run. No one had ever done that before.

IF YOU LIKE HOME RUNS, THEN BRADY ANDERSON IS A BETTER CHOICE ...

... because he did things that no one ever believed a leadoff hitter could do. In his first year at the top of the Baltimore lineup, Anderson (LEFT) had more than 20 homers and 50 stolen bases. In 1995, he stole 34 bases in a row. In 1996, Anderson set another record by leading off four straight games with a home run. He finished the season with 50 homers. Buford hit 67 for Baltimore—in five years!

FRANK ROBINSON WAS BETTER THAN BROOKS ROBINSON …

… because he turned a good Orioles team into a great one. Baltimore never finished higher than second before 1966. After Frank Robinson arrived, they won the pennant four times—in 1966, 1969, 1970, and 1971. He hit 179 home runs during his six seasons with the team. He also batted better than .300 four times and was named the AL MVP in 1966.

HITTING IS ONLY HALF THE STORY. BROOKS ROBINSON WAS BETTER THAN FRANK ROBINSON …

… because he probably saved as many runs with his glove as he drove in with his bat. With Brooks Robinson at third, Baltimore pitchers never feared balls hit to the "hot corner." He speared line drives, fielded bunts one-handed, and turned hard grounders into easy outs. Brooks Robinson played his entire career for the Orioles—23 seasons in all—and was elected to the Hall of Fame in 1983.

ABOVE: Frank and Brooks Robinson shared the cover of this guidebook in 1967.

The great Browns and Orioles teams and players have left their marks on the record books. These are the "best of the best" ...

⚾ ORIOLES AWARD WINNERS

BOOG POWELL   outfield

Boog Powell

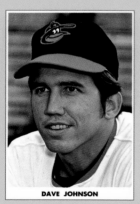

DAVE JOHNSON

Davey Johnson

WINNER	AWARD	YEAR
Roy Sievers	Rookie of the Year	1949*
Ron Hansen	Rookie of the Year	1960
Brooks Robinson	Most Valuable Player	1964
Curt Blefary	Rookie of the Year	1965
Brooks Robinson	All-Star Game MVP	1966
Frank Robinson	Most Valuable Player	1966
Frank Robinson	World Series MVP	1966
Mike Cuellar	Cy Young Award	1969
Boog Powell	Most Valuable Player	1970
Brooks Robinson	World Series MVP	1970
Frank Robinson	All-Star Game MVP	1971
Jim Palmer	Cy Young Award	1973
Al Bumbry	Rookie of the Year	1973
Jim Palmer	Cy Young Award	1975
Jim Palmer	Cy Young Award	1976
Eddie Murray	Rookie of the Year	1977
Mike Flanagan	Cy Young Award	1979
Steve Stone	Cy Young Award	1980
Cal Ripken Jr.	Rookie of the Year	1982
Cal Ripken Jr.	Most Valuable Player	1983
Rick Dempsey	World Series MVP	1983
Gregg Olson	Rookie of the Year	1989
Frank Robinson	Manager of the Year	1989
Cal Ripken Jr.	Most Valuable Player	1991
Cal Ripken Jr.	All-Star Game MVP	1991
Davey Johnson	Manager of the Year	1997
Roberto Alomar	All-Star Game MVP	1998
Cal Ripken Jr.	All-Star Game MVP	2001
Miguel Tejada	All-Star Game MVP	2005

Team played as St. Louis Browns

ACHIEVEMENT	YEAR
AL Pennant Winner	1944*
AL Pennant Winner	1966
World Series Champions	1966
AL East Champions	1969
AL Pennant Winner	1969
AL East Champions	1970
AL Pennant Winner	1970
World Series Champions	1970
AL East Champions	1971
AL Pennant Winner	1971
AL East Champions	1973
AL East Champions	1974
AL East Champions	1979
AL Pennant Winner	1979
AL East Champions	1983
AL Pennant Winner	1983
World Series Champions	1983
AL Wild Card	1996
AL East Champions	1997

Team played as St. Louis Browns

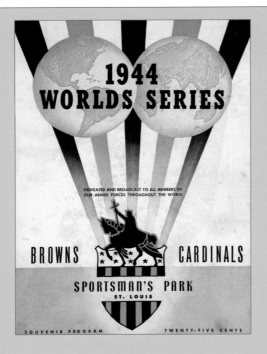

ABOVE: Roberto Alomar batted .333 for the 1997 team.
LEFT: This program was sold at the 1944 World Series.

43

PINPOINTS

The history of a baseball team is made up of many smaller stories. These stories take place all over the map—not just in the city a team calls "home." Match the pushpins on these maps to the **TEAM FACTS**, and you will begin to see the story of the Orioles unfold!

TEAM FACTS

1 Baltimore, Maryland—*The team has played here since 1954.*

2 New York, New York—*Jim Palmer was born here.*

3 Pikesville, Kentucky—*Mark Reynolds was born here.*

4 Billings, Montana—*Dave McNally was born here.*

5 Inglewood, California—*Scott McGregor was born here.*

6 St. Louis, Missouri—*The team played here as the Browns from 1902 to 1953.*

7 Little Rock, Arkansas—*Brooks Robinson was born here.*

8 Beaumont, Texas—*Frank Robinson was born here.*

9 Lakeland, Florida—*Boog Powell was born here.*

10 Seattle, Washington—*Cal Ripken Jr. won the 2001 All-Star Game MVP here.*

11 Havana, Cuba—*Rafael Palmeiro was born here.*

12 Agua Negras, Venezuela—*Melvin Mora was born here.*

Rafael Palmeiro

GLOSSARY

🧠 **AL EAST**—A group of American League teams that play in the eastern part of the country.

🧠 **ALL-STAR GAME**—Baseball's annual game featuring the best players from the American League and National League.

🧠 **AMERICAN LEAGUE (AL)**—One of baseball's two major leagues; the AL began play in 1901.

🧠 **AMERICAN LEAGUE CHAMPIONSHIP SERIES (ALCS)**—The playoff series that has decided the American League pennant since 1969.

🧠 **ASSISTS**—Throws that lead to an out.

🧠 *CIRCUMFERENCE*—The distance around an object.

🧠 **COMPLETE GAME**—A game started and finished by the same pitcher.

🧠 **CY YOUNG AWARD**—The award given each year to each league's best pitcher.

🧠 *DECADES*—Periods of 10 years; also specific periods, such as the 1950s.

🧠 *GENERATIONS*—Periods of years roughly equal to the time it takes for a person to be born, grow up, and have children.

🧠 **GRAND SLAM**—A home run with the bases loaded.

🧠 **HALL OF FAME**—The museum in Cooperstown, New York, where baseball's greatest players are honored.

🧠 **KNUCKLEBALLS**—Pitches thrown with no spin, which "wobble" as they near home plate.

🧠 *LOGO*—A symbol or design that represents a company or team.

🧠 **MOST VALUABLE PLAYER (MVP)**—The award given each year to each league's top player; an MVP is also selected for the World Series and the All-Star Game.

🧠 **PENNANT**—A league championship. The term comes from the triangular flag awarded to each season's champion, beginning in the 1870s.

🧠 **ROOKIE OF THE YEAR**—The annual award given to each league's best first-year player.

🧠 **RUNS BATTED IN (RBIs)**—A statistic that counts the number of runners a batter drives home.

🧠 **SHUTOUT**—A game in which one team does not score a run.

🧠 *STRATEGY*—A plan or method for succeeding.

🧠 **SWITCH-HITTER**—A player who can hit from either side of home plate.

🧠 *TRADITION*—A belief or custom that is handed down from generation to generation.

🧠 **TRIPLE CROWN**—An honor given to a player who leads the league in home runs, batting average, and RBIs.

🧠 *WORLD WAR II*—The war between the major powers of Europe, Asia, and North America that lasted from 1939 to 1945. The United States entered the war in 1941.

EXTRA INNINGS

TEAM SPIRIT introduces a great way to stay up to date with your team! Visit our **EXTRA INNINGS** link and get connected to the latest and greatest updates. **EXTRA INNINGS** serves as a young reader's ticket to an exclusive web page—with more stories, fun facts, team records, and photos of the Orioles. Content is updated during and after each season. The **EXTRA INNINGS** feature also enables readers to send comments and letters to the author! Log onto:

www.norwoodhousepress.com/library.aspx

and click on the tab: **TEAM SPIRIT** to access **EXTRA INNINGS**.

Read all the books in the series to learn more about professional sports. For a complete listing of the baseball, basketball, football, and hockey teams in the **TEAM SPIRIT** series, visit our website at:

www.norwoodhousepress.com/library.aspx

ON THE ROAD

BALTIMORE ORIOLES
333 West Camden Street
Baltimore, Maryland 21201
(888) 848-2473
baltimore.orioles.mlb.com

NATIONAL BASEBALL
HALL OF FAME AND MUSEUM
25 Main Street
Cooperstown, New York 13326
(888) 425-5633
www.baseballhalloffame.org

ON THE BOOKSHELF

To learn more about the sport of baseball, look for these books at your library or bookstore:

- Augustyn, Adam (editor). *The Britannica Guide to Baseball*. New York, NY: Rosen Publishing, 2011.

- Dreier, David. *Baseball: How It Works*. North Mankato, MN: Capstone Press, 2010.

- Stewart, Mark. *Ultimate 10: Baseball*. New York, NY: Gareth Stevens Publishing, 2009.

INDEX

ABOUT THE AUTHOR

MARK STEWART has written more than 50 books on baseball and over 150 sports books for kids. He grew up in New York City during the 1960s rooting for the Yankees and Mets, and was lucky enough to meet players from both teams. Mark comes from a family of writers. His grandfather was Sunday Editor of *The New York Times,* and his mother was Articles Editor of *Ladies' Home Journal* and *McCall's.* Mark has profiled hundreds of athletes over the past 25 years. He has also written several books about his native New York and New Jersey, his home today. Mark is a graduate of Duke University, with a degree in history. He lives and works in a home overlooking Sandy Hook, New Jersey. You can contact Mark through the Norwood House Press website.